Poetry doesn't come to me anymore

Swaty Prakash

India | USA | UK

Presentation by *BookLeaf Publishing*

Web: www.bookleafpub.com

E-mail: info@bookleafpub.com

ISBN: 9789363311879

First edition 2024

For Dhaani because by just being her, she lets me be.

ACKNOWLEDGEMENT

Poetry doesn't come in isolation. At least, to me, it came amid chaos and crowd. When I couldn't understand the whys and the hows, poetry came to help me calm. When I wanted to howl (which I often did) poetry came to me and helped.

And then a few very important people who helped me carve my words into this form.
My father, without whom I would have never known the depths, neither mine nor the world's; and the shallowness (of people, situations and emotions).
My Mumma, who continues to teach me about life, love and a few curries too.
My Manas, who is the reason I know the difference between 'have' and 'have not.'
The many friends who have stayed with me, despite me being me.
And my life, which honestly has been my constant companion in this poetic journey, quite literally!

Under the Carpet

It is not all dirt under the carpet.
There are some hidden memories too
The ones, that are precious, but not pious
Probably, precious 'cause not pious.
Maybe some days are tucked in too,
when someone had spat venom or truth.
Or maybe both.
That's what is under the carpet—
Ugly, uncensored versions of truths nobody
should know,
Broken pieces of mirror with images, sharp,
distorted and nameless.
Under the carpet is everything a life hides to
live.
Mine looks red and hides black, even gray.
And under my carpet is also the day I dared say
"I give up"
I obviously slid it in and brushed it with colors
of strength.
But that day is right there!

I don't say it loud or often
but one day, I might just pick it up,
dust off the fear and scrape off that paint.
One day I might wear it too.
Until then, the carpet stays beautiful. And red.

From Behind Closed Doors

Every house has some laughters
You need to press your ears really hard to hear
them though.
And you need to not rush the pain or hush the
tales.
Between the dry, cold stirring of utensils and
people,
Amid the yells and screams, you will hear the
giggles, suppressed snorts too.
But you need to stay longer.
There will surely be sobs and whimpers
And every possible silent churning that you
mapped in your head
But these are the tales of the dark when no one's
spared.
Sorry, I digress.
So, treat every house like it's a survivor and not
a tragedy
And though you may see initial gloom, wait a
little longer

'Cause while they were braving the storm
They were drenched, exhilarated like on swings.
And remember, even if some boats drown eventually,
rocking boats can still make stomachs tickle.

Death of a Poet

Poetry doesn't come to me anymore

Truths ink my soul in black
Lies, some moons ago, gave way to life.
Smothered by the aging sun
Parched words are no more in fancy fonts or
screeching colors
They read like frown lines, but I can't help
Poetry doesn't come to me anymore.

Paper boats, rubber band rings and origami ships
They weren't just folds and cuts,
They towered our lies, tucked our truths
But lies lie scattered, and truth, all cold and
naked
Poetry doesn't come to me anymore.

Sheets of paper remain blank and ugly
Wasted and torn, my brilliance in haze
But I can't help, I can't cry
Poetry left, left a void
Now, all I have is a confession that Poetry
doesn't come to me anymore.

The Fallen Leaf

The Fallen Leaf

It fell this morning.
Nobody reported a storm.
No one saw a springing teenager from across the
street,
And yet, it lies on the ground
That last leaf.
The one that turned yellow many suns ago
The one that kept twirling and twitching and still
held it all.
It fell.
It was scared that the world would fall too.
The little dying leaf didn't know
We don't fall.
We might always fail but we stay.
Always.

Wait no more!

Shhhhh...
Tiptoe through my mugged life
Lest these wet clingy reds stick to you. Believe
me, they don't wash off easily.
They stay and stink and they laugh sometimes.
Not the companion-partner laugh but the
piercing mocking one.
They don't come cheap or kind.
So shut yourself, and don't smell 'em...

Shhhhh...
Are you waiting still?
Pitying? Worrying? Doubting?
That's always how it traps.
With the guilt.

Will You Really Not Come Back?

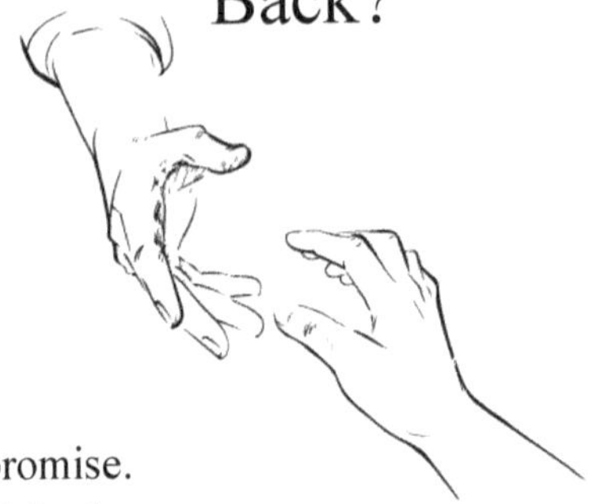

No.
Don't promise.
Don't claim love.
Don't make shiny, sturdy sand castles.
They will, after all, crumble at the slightest
touch.
Nothing you offer doesn't quiver.
Neither your lips nor our dreams.
But before the castle is one with the sea
Before your love starts to shiver
Come back one more time.
Come back because I still haven't told you the
last line of my poem.
Come back because we still haven't soaked in
each other's existence
Come back because your absence still leaves
that space.
Come back because we still haven't breathed in
each other's love
Come back because I haven't told you why I
hate you.

My Little Corner

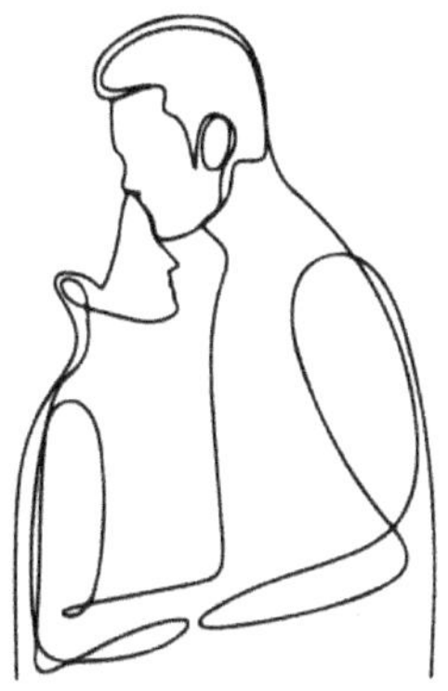

Between right and wrong
you and me
beginning and end
lies a small space.
That space is mine
that space I want to claim
that space is where I breathe and live,
without the struggle of being right or the fear of
being wrong
where I can melt and you can take shape
where my end begins and yet the beginning
doesn't end.
Meet me, in that space.

When Forever Becomes Reality

Years ago
When he promised me forever
and spelt out his vows,
I laughed.
I laughed because I thought forever is
impossible and vows can be broken.
Innocent? I know.
I thought the sad part was that none of this
would be true.
Innocent, I indeed was.
And the sad part is all of it comes true!

My Daughter

My precious one
I may never warn you again
but today should be enough to keep you away
from my darkness.
Remember, my burdens are mine to bear,
Failures, mine to face alone,
Successes may be yours to cherish, but mine to
burden.

None of this belongs to you, my love,
None of this should weigh on your grace,
Step forward or perhaps step aside.

Don't let me fool you into owning any of this, or
any of me.

Inviting Nightmares

Tonight when I sleep
I should not dream.
Tonight I should fight my demons
and breathe in my nightmares.
Dreams make it all so beautiful
Dreams make it all so unreal
Dreams make reality look ugly
Dreams make reality too real.
Tonight when I sleep
I should just see my life.

My Backpack of Questions

My bag full of questions,
Of the whys, hows, whens, and wheres
Why doesn't it ever burst?
When I stop by for a cup of tea,
Why doesn't that old thief take it away with
him?
Why can I not burn these questions into ashes,
scatter them from the cliff
and come back
Light, without seeking answers and accepting
everything life gives?
Soaked in rain, why doesn't this bag ever find a
hole and lighten me too?
Maybe I will never know.

Yet I am all!

I am not a cheerful song,
Nor am I the sudden joy of meeting old
acquaintances.
I am not even the sweet exhaustion of a Holi
afternoon,
Nor am I the last line of a poem discovered after
long sleepless nights.

I am not the innocence of laughter in the rain,
Nor do I play hide-and-seek with wrinkles in
playful abandon.
I am neither the myths that make lovers' rhymes,
Nor the arrogance hidden in tears of victory.

I am none of these, yet I am all.
I am you.
And you.
I'm but a mirror, reflecting your true call.

Need No Anchor

They talk like anchor is a good thing to have.
To be.
Like being tied to a weight
being a weight.
Like being stifled
or stifling
makes you better.
Anchor is not what I want to be
Anchor is not what I want.

I Don't Show

When they pat my back
smile and nod
when they cheer me aloud
or stand by my side
when they tell me they are proud.
I crack.
But I don't show.
I melt within
But, of course, I don't show.
Like a big slab of ice,
when hammered
stays frozen.
But fissures and cracks like threads of water
spread within
Ice doesn't show.
Till it melts,
Ice remains ice.

A Call from Nowhere

Sometimes, when I look back
I see a girl smiling at me
waving and pacing towards me.
Sometimes when I look back
she calls my name
and pants as she runs.
Towards me.
But that is just sometimes.
On days when I miss her or want her to call me
she remains lost, hidden.
She tricks me, I feel.
Like everything else, she comes to me when I
need her no more.

For Dhaani, my beautiful one!

You amaze me my little one.
Your wit, your beauty compel me to claim you
My heart may wander
and tell me lies.
My eyes may shut close to every nuance that
tells me how you bloom on your own.
I may just look at your eyes and claim they look
like mine
or that the dimples look like his.
But those dreams are yours and yours alone
and that glimmer of smile
that spreads on your face and around...
all that is yours..
Yes, you are mine
and yet
my presence cannot define

Your exquisite shine.
You share my genes, my memories
and yet
my share in your life is not whole, but just a part
of your many beautiful stories.

I am from...

I am from the trodden mountain treks and the
unexplored by lanes of a small city
from naphthalene balls tucked in trunks and
monkey caps that were funk
I am from the reality of soggy paper boats and
newspapers that were once sold
I am from scooping custard layer by layer and
Choco bars that are now not so rare
I am from rented comics and dreams of 3D
From English novels that were translated into
Hindi
I am from fake bravery and shy smiles
from "joint" family ties that grew distant by
miles and miles
I am from a budgeted childhood and calculated
risks
from dreams and realities that I thought, could
never mix

I am from youthful camps and first-ever passport
stamp
from growing up lighting many a lamp
I am from happiness, beliefs and expectations,
from a lot of hurdles and various failed factions.
I am from hope and despair
and curiosity for everything that was rare.

Let Me Lie a Little

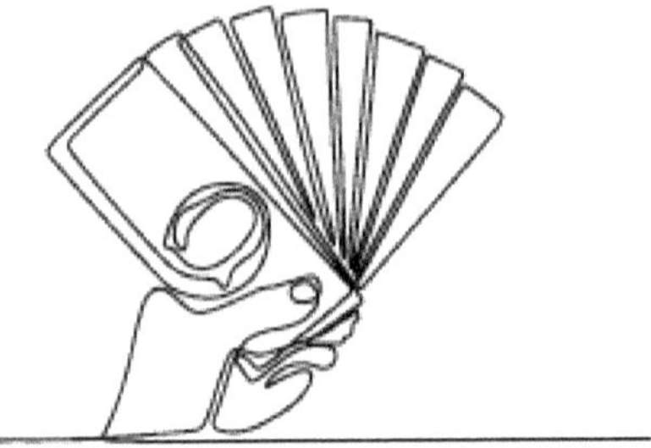

I like truths.
Who doesn't?
But there are some lies that make truths look
dull and sad.
I like those lies better!
They string together my thoughts, adorn them
with flowers
and leave me lighter, happier
even if delusional.
Lies aren't that bad, I feel
they may not be the final deal
but when nothing else works
that's when lies help
make truth a little more bearable.
And facts give way to a little fiction and lend a
hand when the feet feel stuck.

My Days

Some days, when I wake up late
when nothing drives me, neither duty nor fate.
When my morning cup of tea can meet the
afternoon coffee
when I can look in the mirror
smile and pause
and still call myself beautiful...
when my day slips into the night
without any hurry in sight
when my sleep and sweat are not in fight,
those are my days.
These are the days I steal from my calendar,
far and few
but they are mine
and they are the reason.
They are the reason the other many, many days
become easy and livable, despite their tricks and
ways.

When Grief Strikes

It pounces on me when I am least expecting it
In the middle of a party, when I throw my head
laughing
it gags me.
Just when I am tasting that last slice of
cheesecake
it slurps through my throat and almost chokes
me with bittersweet memories.
Grief, when I cry
eludes me.
Grief when I am alone often stays afar too.
It leaps and greets when I least expect it
It sneaks up on me and hugs me
sometimes I feel exhausted and trapped
but often it comes with an air of comfort and a
sense of belonging.
Grief, you don't bother me anymore!

Where it still made sense!

Between reality and that day lies a blank space
where I haven't yet answered the phone.
In that space, a fancy fruit platter lies untouched,
and the leftover dinner from yesterday is not
cold.
Between that moment and the moment when that
wasn't
I am still a hopeful alive being.
That is where I am still alive.

In the Waiting Room

When the visiting hour ends
We look at each other
And smile.
Not the happy, 'I am fine' smile.
'I survived' smile.

After the day-long facade of gratitude and hope,
When the waiting hour ends
We cry,
In grief and hopelessness.
And in relief too.

During the long, endless pit of nights
When they announce 'Bed No. 4'
Each one looks and prays.

Except for that young man,
For everyone else, it is yet another save.

In the Waiting Room
When Bed No. 2 and 3 exchange a glance
There is a hidden nod of assurance, of relief.

As Bed No. 4 is called
Everyone waits, pretends to stay asleep
And the room stinks of helplessness and guilt.

Dreams She Lived

She checked her to-do list
Everything she wanted was now in her fist.
The chase had got her all
There were victories, even though scars of a few
bruises reminded her of the falls
And yet
While she lived her dreams,
It was her life she lost.

'Happy Anniversary'

He posed.
She smiled.
He clicked.
She posted and counted the friends who liked.
Funny, in that world
Nothing is gray or blurred.
The story here, in this world, is different.
Here,
they are once again
Lonely and alone in their togetherness.